A S S

ASSEMBLY

NOVICA TADIĆ

TRANSLATED FROM THE SERBIAN BY

STEVEN TEREF & MAJA TEREF

HOST PUBLICATIONS
AUSTIN, TEXAS

TABLE OF CONTENTS

Introduction: The Birdman of Belgrade i

Translators' Note: Chasing the Mockerator & Other Monsters ix

Translating Tadić 1

I

ЦРВЕНИ СКАКАВАЦ 4
RED LOCUST 5

СКЛОНИШТЕ, ВАШ 6
SHELTER, LOUSE 7

ПАРАМПАРЧАД 8
SMITHEREENS 9

ЦИПЕЛЕ ЦИПЕЛИЦЕ 10
SHOES, TINY SHOES 11

ТЕШКОЋА 12
DIFFICULTY 13

УОБРАЖЕЊЕ 14
A CONCEIT 15

ЉУДИ КОЈИ КРЕШТЕ 16

PEOPLE WHO SHRIEK 17

ЗАСПАХ ДА МЕ ПРОЂЕ СТРАВА 18

I FELL ASLEEP TO WAIT OUT MY DREAD 19

ПОСЛЕ БЕСАНЕ НОЋИ 20

AFTER A SLEEPLESS NIGHT 21

ПРЕД ОГЛЕДАЛОМ 22

IN FRONT OF THE MIRROR 23

ВЕЛИКО БЛАТО 24

VELIKO BLATO 25

II

ТАМНЕ СТВАРИ 28

DARK THINGS 29

МАСКЕ 30

MASKS 31

МАЧКА 40

THE CAT 41

РОДОСЛОВ ЏЕЛАТА 42
THE GENEALOGY OF THE EXECUTIONER 43

РЕСИЦА, МИНИФОН 46
UVULA, BUGGING DEVICE 47

ЈАБУКА 48
AN APPLE 49

МУВА, 1989. 50
FLY, 1989. 51

ОКУПАЦИЈА 52
OCCUPATION 53

ИЗМЕЂУ ДВЕ САЛВЕ 54
BETWEEN TWO SALVOS 55

БИОГРАФИЈА 56
BIOGRAPHY 57

КОНГРЕС (ФАНТАЗМА) 58
ASSEMBLY (PHANTASM) 59

СТРАХ 60
FEAR 61

БРОЈАНИЦА (ПРОТИВ УТВАРА) 62
INCANTATIONS (AGAINST PHANTOMS) 63

III

ИЗЛОЖБА 66
EXHIBITION 67

ЗАСТАВА 68
FLAG 69

ФОТОГРАФИЈА 70
THE PHOTOGRAPH 71

СВЕСКА, ГЛАС 72
NOTEBOOK, VOICE 73

УДОВИЦА 74
THE WIDOW 75

ЈА И ТИ 76
YOU AND I 77

СОНЕТ МРТВИХ СОВА 78
SONNET OF DEAD OWLS 79

IV

КЕЗИЛОВ ДОЛАЗАК 82
MOCKERATOR'S ARRIVAL 83

ИЗА РУЖИЧЊАКА КЕЗИЛО 84
MOCKERATOR BEHIND THE ROSE GARDEN 85

КЕЗИЛОВА ПОЈАВА НА ПРСТИМА 86
MOCKERATOR'S APPEARANCE ON FINGERS 87

ФЛАША КЕЗИЛО 88
BOTTLE-MOCKERATOR 89

БОКАЛ КЕЗИЛО 90
PITCHER-MOCKERATOR 91

ЛОНАЦ КЕЗИЛО 92
POT-MOCKERATOR 93

ЈАБУКА ЈЕ КЕЗИЛОВА 94
EVEN THE APPLE BELONGS TO THE MOCKERATOR 95

ПОРЦУЛАН КЕЗИЛО 96
PORCELAIN-MOCKERATOR 97

СПАЛА ЈЕ САПУНИЦА 98
SOAPSUDS SLID OFF 99

У ПОСУЂУ КЕЗИЛО 100
MOCKERATOR IN THE DISHES 101

КЕЗИЛИЋИ 102
NEWBORN MOCKERATORS 103

СМРТ У СТОЛИЦИ 104
DEATH IN THE CHAIR 105

V

AB OVO 112
AB OVO 113

РИТУАЛ 114
RITUAL 115

КОКОТУША 116
CLUCKER 117

КОКОШ У СОБИ 118
HEN IN THE ROOM 119

ГЛЕДАМ 120
AS I WATCH 121

РАДНИ СТО 122
DESK 123

БОР 124
PINE TREE 125

СТОЛЊАК 126
TABLECLOTH 127

ЗАВЕСЕ 128
CURTAINS 129

НАХТКАСНА 130
NIGHTSTAND 131

ЛУТАЈУЋИ ОГАЊ 132
WANDERING FIRE 133

СВЕЋА 134
CANDLE 135

BIBLIOGRAPHY 136

INTRODUCTION

THE BIRDMAN OF BELGRADE

Meeting Novica Tadić is like walking into one of his poems.

On a summer evening in 2005, Maja and I visited Novica at his attic apartment for the first time. His residence, a gray five story building without an elevator, located in the Belgrade municipality of Zemun, is where he still lives with his wife and daughter. Although Zemun is a charming historical part of the city overlooking the Danube, at the time, it struck me as a remote and foreboding place of imposing, graffiti-smothered concrete buildings behind which concealed teenagers whispered in unlit gangways and courtyards, the orange tips of their cigarettes occasionally arcing in the darkness.

As we climbed the dimly lit marble steps, we passed by seemingly forgotten unplugged appliances randomly placed on the landings: a washing machine, a refrigerator, a stove. A bespectacled middle-aged woman with black hair carrying cigarettes silently studied us as she descended the stairway. We later discovered that the woman was Novica's wife going out for a smoke.

Novica's daughter greeted us at the entrance and led us into the living room where Novica waited for us. Behind him, the slanted wood-paneled walls framed open skylight windows that let in rectangles of night and the desperate, cacophonous calls of invisible gulls. At the time of our first visit, I had been reading Bruno Schultz's *The Street of Crocodiles* and couldn't shake the feeling that I had walked into the aviary attic of the narrator's father. In the corner of the living room, a small silent TV showed a hypnotism program with a near-comatose mumbling woman slumped in a chair.

This is where the Gothic story ends.

There is a more meaningful darkness at play – no *Castle of Otranto* here.

A successful poet at the peak of his career and poetic powers, Novica exudes a disarmingly self-deprecating manner. One would think that a poet such as Tadić, whose work is so often grim, would be brooding at best; however, Novica has always been cheery and quick with a joke, sometimes at his own expense. While arranging to meet him for the first time, he humorously replied that it might be difficult to see him during the day because he was a vampire lurking in the shadows. He was anything but. In fact, not only did our initial meeting take place on a bright summer morning, but Novica spent the whole day taking us around to art galleries along Knez Mihailova Street and to his favorite café tucked away in the shaded courtyard of the Serbian Literary Society where he treated us to apricot juice. In his avuncular manner, he acted more as a tour guide than a prestigious award-winning poet.

Indeed, every time Maja and I visit Novica, he magnanimously plies us with various works of Serbian literature. Once, at his apartment, while sipping homemade currant juice and discussing the underrepresentation of women poets from the Balkans in translation, Novica left the room only to reappear with a stack of books by Serbian women poets as a present for us.

Despite Novica's approachable and witty manner, tremendous generosity, and warm hospitality, I often think back to that first evening and how much the environment surrounding us resembled the atmosphere and trappings of his poems. Was I simply projecting my impressions of his poetry onto the man himself? Was I cultifying the nightmarian poet? Perhaps. It's difficult not to.

Novica Tadić's poetry is, at times, oppressively hellish though it is not gratuitous nor without precedent. In one of his most disturbing poems, "Shoes, Tiny Shoes," the implication is that the speaker tortures and kills a little girl after taking her to the movies. The violation itself is left unspoken since the implicit crime has been excised from the middle of the poem; namely, the girl, who is directly addressed as "you" for most of the poem is suddenly and inexplicably referred to as "she," i.e. in the third person, in the conclusion.

Unseemly though it may be, the poem is heir to more sinister work. In the "Third Canto" of Comte de Lautremont's *Maldoror*, the title character rapes, mutilates, and kills a little girl (Lautremont 114-5). In Gottfried Benn's "Happy Youth," the speaker coolly describes how rats had nested and fed upon the corpse of a girl (lines 1-5, 7-9). Unlike these predecessors of "Shoes, Tiny Shoes," a moral anchors the poem as the sound of the girl's shoes "tapping" under the bed at night haunts the speaker-killer. Thus, the poem has more in common with Edgar Allen Poe's "The Tell-tale Heart" in that in both pieces the conscience of each murderer betrays him at the end than with the morality-baiting Maldoror.

Many of Tadić's poems contain dramas of victimization. Either a character, such as the woman in "Red Locust," or the speaker, as in "You and I," is being victimized. Why is this dynamic such a prevalent theme in Tadić's verse? Early in our correspondence with him, while inquiring about his influences, I asked whether his work was informed by the likes of Trakl and other sundry morbid types. Instead of answering the question directly, Tadić tersely stated that his biggest influence was Communism (email 5/9/04). Later, during our first meeting, while sitting in an outdoor café in downtown Belgrade, he elaborated on his earlier response by recounting two horrid encounters with members of Yugoslavia's Communist regime during which he was severely beaten. The first beating took place in his youth when soldiers attacked him for crossing a field where they had set up camp. Tadić was beaten a second time, on this occasion severely, by Milošević's militia during the initially peaceful 1999 protests against the dictator. He underscored his point by taking Maja's hand and placing it against his misshapen ribs. These victimizations, he emphasized, permanently marked his life and subsequently his work. Indeed, finding overt political references in the poet's work is not difficult for a critical reader. The death of Tito (Yugoslavia's founding Communist dictator) is explicitly referenced in "Between Two Salvos" and obliquely present in "Masks." Other bold political poems criticizing Communist rule are "An Apple," in which a fighter jet contrail is equated with the signature of a dictator, and "Biography," in which the speaker is beaten up by the police for no apparent reason. All of these poems challenge the oppressive nature of existing in a Communist country.

Whether addressing political concerns or deep psychological horrors, a ceaseless parade of monsters and other strange creatures frequently punctuate the dramas unfolding in Tadić's poetry: a red locust, insectoid manuscripts, an assortment of apparitions, and a monstrous moth, to name but a few. The foreignness of the more elaborate figures accentuates the terror of the speaker's perceived experience. In the *Mockerators* cycle, an unnamed guilt or other psychological trigger, manifested in the ever-shifting guise of the mockerators, plagues the speaker: "Guilt, gather giblets / beneath the fresh mound" ("Mockerator's Arrival").

Even when Tadić features recognizable animals, they often have a threatening or haunting presence in his verse. Of these, birds and birdlike creatures are the most frequent figures, such as ghostly owls in the concrete poem "Sonnet of Dead Owls" or the "bird-faced specter" in "Exhibition." But, the hen, the most ominous bird in all of Tadić's oeuvre, reigns supreme in his horror-verse. At times, hens may be a subtle sinister presence, as in "Occupation," however, the hen as an archetype of oppression blazes in "Ab Ovo" and "Hen in the Room."

Why the obsession with monsters, both familiar and not? The clue to this question, I believe, can be found in "Smithereens" in which the speaker mocks a "secondary god" over the idea of "creation." Who is this inferior deity and what kind of creation is implied? In an email exchange with the poet, Tadić clarified that the reference was to Bogomilism, a heretical medieval Christian cult that once existed in what is now Bosnia. The God of the Bogomils, according to Tadić, was the "janitor" of the physical world created by Satanael, his first son (email 5/5/04).

"Smithereens" thus highlights the monstrousness of living in a demonically imperfect world referred to as a "divine armpit." As it were, Tadić confided to us that he sees himself as a "Bogomil" living in a hopeless world subjugated to the vicissitudes of unholy forces. Case in point, even his latest book *Devil's Companion* (2008) reaffirms his belief in who is at the helm.

Bogomilism has figured as a subject in relation to Serbian poetry, however rarely. Though the dualistic religion has occasionally cropped up in the poetry of both Vasko Popa and poet and translator of Serbian poetry John Matthias, Tadić's poetry fully embraces Bogomilism as his metaphoric foundation. According to *Medieval Heresy*, in one version of the Bogomil creation myth, Satanael, in a Promethean gesture, stole the soul from God and shoved it down Adam's throat. However, for the divine energy to remain anchored in the body, Satanael "vomited into Adam's mouth unclean creatures that would sully the soul and keep it prisoner in the body" (Lambert 20-21). The Bogomil creation story is all the more apropos in Tadić's work considering that the collection containing "Smithereens" is allusively titled *Maw*, written in the wake of Tito's reign.

Bogomilism contextualizes much of the strangeness in Tadić's poetry and goes far in explaining his poetics. Working within this historic framework, the poet gives himself a rich poetic palette from which to address a wide range of personal and public concerns. Given such a context, he can hide in public without appearing to do so, thereby avoiding government scrutiny. At his most effective, Tadić can give voice to any subversive political sentiments. Instead of writing a poem openly defiant against political intrusiveness and running the risk of being censored, he writes a weird poem about a "ghost" attaching a listening device to the uvula of a "geezer-starling," as he does in "Uvula, Bugging Device," the placement of the intrusive device in the mouth, of course, not being arbitrary.

Furthermore, this idea of spiritual pollution has continued in his work. In "Notebook, Voice," from the 2006 collection *The Unknown*, the speaker idly writes "People are impure creatures." This statement in and of itself possesses little dramatic force, however, in the larger context of Bogomilism within Tadić's poetics, this simple sentence bursts with allusive power.

Additionally, religious and spiritual ideas, heretical and otherwise, figure as more than a convenient conceit for Tadić. He, at times, earnestly addresses religious and spiritual concerns, especially in his later work. In "Candle," the speaker unabashedly views religion as a safe harbor without a trace of irony. During one of our visits, Novica gave us a beautiful box set of Serbian religious writings admitting that he drew inspiration from them. One of the books, *Time and Eternity: An Anthology of Serbian Prayers: 13th-*

20ᵗʰ Century, he was proud to point out, included "Make Haste, Mild One, Help Me (Prayer from the Darkness)," a prose poem from his 2001 collection *Shelter* (244).

Novica Tadić's lyric impulse follows closest in the footsteps of Serbia's most widely revered poet Vasko Popa. Popa, a lyric poet known for fortifying the myths of Serbian history and its heroes, often reconciled Slavic pagan imagery with Eastern Orthodox heritage and used this blending of traditions as a template to showcase the strength of the human spirit. Tadić, despite his more recent religious tendencies, often dismantles the conventional cultural myths and undermines them by frequently creating a kind of anti-mythos exhibiting human weakness, cruelty, and suffering.

The original 1981 edition of *Maw* was initially structured according to thematically-linked lyric cycles, much in the vein of Popa. In one such cycle, *Shelters*, Tadić infuses the idea of shelter with an unforgiving irony. The house in "Red Locust" does not protect its owner, a woman who has been victimized by the speaker in the poem. In "Shoes, Tiny Shoes," the adult speaker, instead of protecting the child in the poem, tortures and kills the little girl. The "secondary god" in the pivot poem "Smithereens" is unable to provide divine shelter for the speaker. In the penultimate poem "Shelter, Louse," the speaker is in what appears to be a bomb shelter in which the only ray of hope seems to be a louse. The cycle ends with "Difficulty" in which the speaker comforts the personified difficulty as opposed to being comforted from difficulty. Though tightly linked by theme, a possible comparison to Popa, Tadić manages to eschew much of the symmetry of his predecessor.

Although Novica Tadić has yet to become as revered in the West as the well-known Popa, he is a renowned poet in his native Serbia. Throughout his career, Novica Tadić has steadily won every major award in Serbia (and former Yugoslavia), such as the Vasko Popa and Desanka Maksimović awards, the latter of which he declined due to that poet's loyalty to the Tito regime. Even with these high profile recognitions of his talent, it has been only with the publication of his last two books *The Unknown* and *Devil's Companion* that his poetry has been cemented in the Serbian literary canon. In 2006, when the textbook publisher Zavod za Udžbenike wanted to modernize its roster of writers, one of the first poets it solicited was Tadić. As exciting as this was, the lynchpin of his career occurred in 2008 when the most prestigious literary press in Serbia, Srpska Književna Zadruga, solicited a book from Tadić which became *Devil's Companion*. In an ironic twist that bemused the poet, the catalog number of the collection was 666!

— *Steven Teref, 2009*

BIBLIOGRAPHY

Lambert, Malcom D. *Medieval Heresy: Popular Movements from Bogomil to Hus*. London: Edward Arnold (Publisher) Ltd., 1977.

Lautreamont, Comte de. Trans. Alexis Lykiard. *Maldoror and the Complete Works of the Comte de Lautreamont*. Cambridge, Massachusetts: Exact Change, 1994.

Miller, David and Stephen Watts, Ed. *Music While Drowning: German Expressionist Poems*. London: Tate Publishing, 2003.

Pejčić, Jovan, Ed. *Vreme i večnost: antologija srpskih molitava: XIII-XX vek*. Novi Sad: Orpheus, 2003.

Tadić, Novica. *Đavolov drug*. Beograd: Srpska književna zadruga, 2008.

—. *Neznan*. Beograd: Zavod za udžbenike, 2006.

—. Personal interview. 5 May, 2004.

—. Personal interview. 9 May, 2004.

—. *Ždrelo*. Beograd: Prosveta, 1981.

TRANSLATORS' NOTE

CHASING THE MOCKERATOR &
OTHER MONSTERS

In July 2008, sitting once more with Novica Tadić in his attic living room, when presented with the final list of the poems to be included in *Assembly*, he noted, "you picked difficult poems." This admission, coming from the poet himself, validated the five years spent in the trenches of interlanguage, the struggle to transport the meaning of the work of the greatest living Serbian poet from no man's land to English language territory.

In compiling *Assembly*, we selected poems spanning Tadić's career, from his first book *Presences* (1974) to *The Unknown* (2006). Our goal was to translate a body of work fully representative of Tadić's poetics, choosing poems that are surreal, lyrical, spiritual, socio-political, urban, grotesque, concrete, abstract, and narrative. Even though Tadić generally writes short lyric poems, we also wanted to represent poems that are long, in cycles, and in sequences. Such an endeavor could not, by its very nature, have been easy, and although many examples could be cited to highlight the challenges of translating Tadić, we will narrow our discussion to but a few.

Section IV of *Assembly*, comprised of a portion of the *Mockerators* cycle from his second book *Death in the Chair* (1975), embodies much of what makes Tadić a difficult poet to translate. It is one of his longest and most complex sequences showcasing a gallery of self-propagating creatures, the *kezila*, or 'mockerators.' This fantastical world, containing an assortment of monsters, exemplifies his linguistic inventions built upon Serbian folkloric tradition, which creates many translational opportunities and solutions (Mikić 135).

For the word *kezilo* (in singular), Tadić took the root of the verb *keziti se*, which means 'to show one's teeth,' 'to make faces (at somebody),' or 'to leer (at somebody),' and married it to *–ilo*, a suffix predominantly reserved for inanimate neuter nouns (Morton 201). By turning *keziti se* into *kezilo* and treating the neologism as an animate noun, Tadić personified the speaker's self-torment. Our one-word solution in English closely follows the original Serbian neologism, a decision driven by practical considerations. Namely, characteristic of this cycle, Tadić created variants of the same monster by forging new noun phrases, many of which consist of the common denominator *kezilo* and a common, inanimate noun or noun phrase, thus forming a hyphenated-sounding construct.

To arrive at a satisfactory translational solution, we analyzed the two morphological units of the word *kezilo*. Both units are actual morphemes in the source language, however, it is their unlikely pairing which poses a challenge for the translator. More specifically, *–ilo* is a suffix mostly, though not exclusively, reserved for inanimate objects, such as, *šilo* ('awl'), *cedilo* ('colander'), *rilo* ('proboscis,' 'snout'), *krilo* ('wing,' 'lap'), and *mastilo* ('ink'). While searching for an adequate solution, we selected the English suffixes '–er' and '–ator' which correspond to the suffix *-ilo* in the source language, guided by two reasons. First, '–ator' is a suffix frequently utilized for inanimate nouns such as 'percolator,' 'refrigerator' or 'accelerator.' Second, '–ator,' when affixed to '–er,' is often used for animate nouns, such as 'moderator' and 'liberator.' This is relevant because, as previously stated, Tadić animates the inanimate noun *kezilo*. As for our treatment of the root word *keziti se*, we selected the verb 'to mock,' which is synonymous with the dictionary definition 'to make faces at.' Thus, we forged our translational equivalent: 'mockerator.'

Tadić frequently utilizes diminutives in his poetry and our challenge as translators was to retain as much of that aspect of his poems while keeping it fresh and meaningful in English. Tadić frequently will use a diminutive in order to accentuate the relative powerlessness of whatever victim is on display in his work. For example, in the eerie poem

"Shoes, Tiny Shoes," a girl is presumably tortured and murdered by the speaker. All that remains of her in the final stanza are her *cipele cipelice*, or, literally, 'shoes, shoelettes' (*sic*) (l.17). In "Red Locust," a woman, who has obviously suffered some recent unspecified trauma, lies on a sofa. A "curtain / billows, brushes against" her *mala ramena*, or 'small shoulders' (ll.5-9). When placed side by side, these diminutive-laden poems would sound flat if we solely used the word 'small' or 'little' which is the literal meaning of Serbian words that end in *–ica* (or its variants) and the word *malo*. Although diminutives in Serbian function much like in English, Tadić's use of diminutives is anything but adorable; each miniaturized object in his verse adds a creepy tone because of the frequent unequal power dynamics at play between the poems' players.

On many occasions, when picking up a new book of poetry translations, a note on the translations is inevitably included, which could be called a defense of translation in which the translator explains the strengths of his or her work. Sometimes, by an artful sleight of hand, the translator confesses that despite his or her triumphs, some aspect of the original poem became 'lost,' such as the rhyme scheme or other form of musicality. In our translations, our Waterloo, such as it is, was found in the poem "Death in the Chair." The seed of the long poem grows out of an untranslatable pun. In Serbian, the word for 'chair' is *stolica*. When this word is "split" in half, it forms two words: *sto* (one hundred) and *lica* (faces) (l.62). This is the central image out of which the entire poem builds itself.

So, what is a translator to do when a pun cannot be carried over into the target language? When faced with this dilemma, the translator has to ask himself or herself whether the poem can survive on its own without the reader's knowledge of the pun. If most poems prosper in anything, it is more often than not on the strength of its images. "Death in the Chair" is replete with powerful images. Moreover, the images and overall meaning of the poem, separate from the pun itself, still come through in the English. Ultimately, the English reading audience does not need the pun in order to understand the point of the poem.

On a general note, the one liberty we have taken in our translations has been the occasional introduction of punctuation when absent in the original, especially regarding much of Tadić's early work where punctuation was sparse at best. The decision to add this scaffolding to the translations wasn't arrived at arbitrarily. Serbian, being immanently a grammar-based language with its seven grammatical cases, enjoys freedoms that English could only fantasize about. English, with its two noun cases is, on the other hand, a syntax shackled language and as such depends more heavily on punctuation and word order for it to cohere. Serbian, depending on its declensions, has thus contortionist-like flexibility regarding word order since suffixes determine which words are subordinate to which subject. Tadić, notably in his early work, on occasion, has pushed the generous limits of Serbian syntax to *Exorcist* or Cirque du Soleil extremes. To approximate this (never mind find an equivalent) in English, it could be argued, would leave readers questioning the competency of the translators. Even with "normalizing" the syntax, punctuation was a necessary injustice so that the shape of the poems could remain as intact as possible.

Tadić is a complex poet even for educated Serbian readers. Our task as translators has been to maintain the complexity of his work while making it available and, more to the point, comprehensible to an English speaking audience. In so doing, rendering Tadić meaningful while upholding the intricacy of his poetics was not merely a series of challenges to be conquered; rather, it was a scholarly journey necessary to help cement a vital voice into the English language.

– Steven Teref & Maja Teref, 2009

BIBLIOGRAPHY

Benson, Morton and Biljana Šljivić-Šimšić, Eds. *Srpskohrvatsko-engleski rečnik*. Second Edition, revised. Beograd: Proveta, 1981.

Mikić, Radivoje. "Misticizam jezika u poeziji Novice Tadića." *Skakutani i kezila*. Tadić, Novica. Beograd: Narodna Knjiga / Alfa, 2002. 127-136.

Tadić, Novica. *Skakutani i kezila*. Beograd: Narodna Knjiga / Alfa, 2002.

Tadić, Novica. *Ždrelo*. Banja Luka: Zadužbina Petar Kočić, 2002.

ACKNOWLEDGMENTS

We owe our deepest gratitude to the editors of the publications who have supported our translations and believed in Novica Tadić's vision.

The following poems have appeared in these journals:

Absinthe: New European Writing: "Exhibition," "The Widow," "You and I," "Shelter, Louse";

Action Yes: "Masks," "The Cat";

Another Chicago Magazine: "Assembly (Phantasm)," "After a Sleepless Night," "I Fell Asleep to Wait Out My Dread";

Black Clock: "Soapsuds Fell Off";

Circumference: "Hen in the Room";

Court Green: "Dark Things," "The Genealogy of the Executioner";

The Dirty Goat, #19 : "Translating Tadić," "Between Two Salvos," "Biography," "An Apple," "Shoes, Tiny Shoes," "The Photograph";

eXchanges: "People Who Shriek," "Incantation (Against Phantoms)," "Notebook, Voice," "Sonnet of Dead Owls";

Melancholia's Tremulous Dreadlocks: "Uvula, Bugging Device," "A Conceit";

New American Writing: "Red Locust," "Smithereens";

Parthenon West Review: "Difficulty";

6x6: "Mockerator's Appearance on Fingers," "Mockerator Behind the Rose Garden," "Mockerator's Arrival," "Pitcher-mockerator," "Pot-mockerator," "Even the Apple Belongs to the Mockerator."

"The Genealogy of the Executioner" was nominated for a Pushcart Prize.

An early version of Steven's graduate thesis "The Nocturnal Monopoly Within: The Poetry of Novica Tadić," which featured excerpts of numerous poems from this collection, was presented with Maja Teref at *(dis)junctions: Theory Reloaded*, 12th Annual Humanities Conference sponsored by University of California, Riverside. Riverside, CA. April 8th, 2005.

"Chasing the Mockerator: The Translatability of Novica Tadić," which featured excerpts of numerous poems from this collection, was presented at the *Poetry and Translation* conference sponsored by the University of Stirling. Stirling, Scotland. July 19th, 2008.

A heartfelt thanks goes to the following people: Arielle Greenberg, who has been a catalyst, an editor and an avid supporter, without whom this project would never have gotten off the ground; Clayton Eshleman, who provided crucial insights about the translation process; Tony Trigilio and Peter Christensen for helping with the development of the thesis; the organizers and moderators of the *(dis)junctions* and *Poetry and Translation* conferences for accepting and supporting our work on Novica Tadić. A special thank you goes to Novica Tadić himself for he has been indispensable in making this project what it is. He has selflessly answered our questions, provided copies of his books, made critical articles about his work available to us and allowed us to meet with him and his family. We're grateful to our families for their unconditional love and support. Thanks to Saša Marković and his family, and Bata and the Starčević family for their support and help in the early days of this project.

Dedicated to our mothers: Lula and Helen

ASSEMBLY

TRANSLATING TADIĆ

An open window, a book on the nightstand;
a man in a black raincoat looms over
a girl revealed in her sleep,
the red polka-dotted spread
folded back.

I open the door to my sister's room:
Novica Tadić cradles her small body
in his black embrace.
Curtains billow behind him,
admit a chill autumn air.

"When I finish translating your poem
I want you gone."

– Steven Teref

I

ЦРВЕНИ СКАКАВАЦ

Крвавим памуком
испуњено је данас
моје кућно звонце

Поред отвореног прозора
на каучу лежи
опружена измождена згромљена

Прозирна завеса
њише се лако и дотиче јој
мала рамена

Тамо пак тамо
по крововима градским трчи
огромни црвени

Скакавац који ће јој
као последњу траву земље
сву косу исећи

Са полице узимам
њену омиљену књигу
и наглас читам

RED LOCUST

My doorbell
filled today
with bloody cotton

By the window
a woman on the couch
sprawled, stunned, thunder-struck

A sheer curtain
billows, brushes against
her narrow shoulders

There, still there,
across the city roofs
springs an enormous red

locust to nip
off all her hair
like the last grass on earth

From the shelf I take
her favorite book
and read aloud

СКЛОНИШТЕ, ВАШ

Пропасти дивна
пропасти
у блештеће платно
огромно
док нас
родитељски
увијаш све
овде
у ваздушном
гнезду
подземном
једна једина
радост
светла ваш
мили
лако
надвитим
црним зидом

SHELTER, LOUSE

Calamity –
splendid calamity –
while you
envelop us all
with your huge
dazzling canvas, here
in the underground
nest, our sole joy:
a luminous louse
creeps along
the looming
black wall

ПАРАМПАРЧАД

Ваздух је муњина
решетка

    Други боже
    зар ћеш се и ти
    бавити стварањем

Сањам кристал
продужетак
приче

    Јутром
    унутрашња
    муњица
    блесне

Дивовски корак тек
предстоји ми

    У васељени
    у дечијим
    колицима сјајним
    плачем

Под пазухом божијим
у маслачку страшном

SMITHEREENS

The air is lightning's
grid

> You, secondary god,
> aren't really going to concern yourself
> with creation, are you

I dream of crystal,
the continuation
of myth

> In the morning,
> inner lightning

A giant step is still
before me

> Ecumenic
> in a shiny stroller
> I cry

In the divine armpit,
in the terrible dandelion

ЦИПЕЛЕ ЦИПЕЛИЦЕ

После биоскопске представе
одводим те у Рупу
и показујем ти
кофер пун ножева, црне рукавице, маску
свилено уже свилено
муњевиту жицу
пипак прст
иглу зуб
прве животиње сјајну крљушт
чудило
али
жртвицу моју моју милу
ти ниси могла видети
само су пуне
светлости
дневне
њене ципеле ципелице сву ноћ дугу
под креветом
трупкале
тихо

SHOES, TINY SHOES

I take you to the Hole
after the movie
and show you
a suitcase filled with knives,
black gloves, a mask,
rope – silken rope,
lightning cord,
a feeler-finger,
a needle, a tooth, glittering
scales of the first beast,
wonder

But filled
only with daylight
you couldn't see these things,
my dear, dear victim

＊

Her shoes, tiny shoes
tapped
under the bed
through the unending night

11

ТЕШКОЋА

О основној тешкоћи
никоме не говорим;
хиљадугодишњи мољац*
на њој у ладици лежи.

Понекад је узимам у наручје
да смерно плачемо;
понекад јој прилазим
с бокалом пуним свеже воде.

* тај мољац, злато, прст божији
радних има хиљаду усница
пипака, сечива, рила
а његова крилца

танана кад се рашире
усред најдубље ноћи
сву ладицу испуни одједном
светлост чудесна.

DIFFICULTY

I don't talk to anyone
about Difficulty.
A thousand year old moth*
lies atop her in a drawer.

Sometimes I take her into my arms;
meekly, we weep.
Sometimes I bring her a pitcher
of fresh water.

*This precious moth, this divine finger,
has a thousand working little lips,
antennae, blades, proboscises,
and flimsy

outspread wings
in the midst of the deepest night.
The entire drawer suddenly fills with
miraculous light.

УОБРАЖЕЊЕ

Тамо тамо лежи –
За гребеном ваздушним
За завесом кишном
За видиком мртвим –

Једино биће
Које ми је слично
Које ме чека
Које ме дозива

С громаде ваздушне
Кроз завесу кишну
Кроз видик самрли
Које ме дозива

Жива лутка једна
Створ очију округлих
Румених усница
Косе расуте кроз земљу

A CONCEIT

There, over there, she lies —
beyond the looming peak
beyond the curtains of rain
beyond the dead horizon —

the only creature
who's similar to me
who's waiting for me
who's calling me

from the looming peak
through the curtains of rain
through the lifeless view
calling me

a living doll
a creature with round eyes
rosy lips
hair spilling into the earth

ЉУДИ КОЈИ КРЕШТЕ

Људи који креште
увек су ме привлачили.

Они су птице
које неће полетети,
до смрти натоварене
људским костима.

PEOPLE WHO SHRIEK

I am always drawn to
people who shriek.

They are birds
unable to take flight,
burdened till death
by human bones.

ЗАСПАХ ДА МЕ ПРОЂЕ СТРАВА

Заспах да ме проће
страва, али одмах

за гриву се ухватих
црног коња у трку
а ветар неки удари
и поче чупати дрвеће
у невиђеном бесу

и бацати га високо у небо,
  као бакље.

I FELL ASLEEP TO WAIT OUT MY DREAD

I fell asleep to wait out
my dread – suddenly

I seized the mane
of a bolting black horse –
a furious wind
ripped out trees

tossed them skyward
        like torches.

ПОСЛЕ БЕСАНЕ НОЋИ

После бесане ноћи
приђох огледалу и видех
поражавајући резултат.
Видех убледело лице странца,
дубоку тугу у очима његовим.
„Створио сам новог човека“,
пршаптах, намигујући ономе у огледалу.
Вратих се, затим, у кревет,
да се одморим
од добро обављеног ноћног посла.

AFTER A SLEEPLESS NIGHT

After a sleepless night
I greeted a disheartening figure
in the mirror
a stranger's haggard face
with dispirited eyes.
"I have created a new man," I whispered,
winking at the one in the mirror.
I went back to bed
to get some rest
after a night-job well done.

ПРЕД ОГЛЕДАЛОМ

Неки незнанац (у кафани, за столом)
на рубу новина нешто записивао.
Не могу се сетити његовог лика,
већ само непријатног погледања
овчице божје на пашњаку.

Јутрос, пред огледалом док се бријем,
искрсну тај призор однекуд,
и никако да прође. Жилет га однео.

Од старог ћу ожиљка направити чамац
и отпловити далеко у крв и црни жуч.

IN FRONT OF THE MIRROR

A stranger scribbled
in the margins of a newspaper
(at a restaurant table).
I can't recall his face,
only the unpleasant glances
of the divine ewe in his pasture.

This morning, as I shaved in the mirror,
that scene returned – I couldn't shake it.
The razorblade nicked it.

From the old scar, I'll build a boat
and sail away into blood and black bile.

ВЕЛИКО БЛАТО

Еје мочварице. трске и рогоз.
локвањи. лети, лети сива врана.
у барском биљу гњурац ћубасти.
мала бела чапља лови жабу, гута жабу.
високо у грању гнезда птица, њишу се лако.
никога нема. у трулом чамцу. овде. тамо.
нико не јаше јато риба. само господа
кормőрани. само гладне кашикаре.
опевајмо цео предео, све што видимо.
кренимо према отвореним водама.
легнимо заувек.

VELIKO BLATO

Marsh harriers. reeds and cattails.
waterlilies. a gray crow flies and flies.
a great-crested grebe amid the marsh plants.
a young white heron catches and swallows a frog.
bird nests up in the branches sway lightly.
no one there. in the rotten boat. here. there.
nobody herds a school of fish. only genteel
cormorants. only hungry shovelers.
laud the whole landscape, all the eye can see.
march toward open waters.
lie down forever.

Veliko Blato: the name of a geographical area by the Danube

II

ТАМНЕ СТВАРИ

Тамне ствари отварају моје очи,
подижу руку, грче прсте.

Оне су далеко и близу,
иза девет брда
и у станишту скровитом.

Ноћ је њихово царство,
а дан који свиће
огртач од светлости.

Нема снаге која их може поништити,
разрешити или објаснити.

Они остају тамо где су.
У грудима, у срцу из кога шуморе.

DARK THINGS

Dark things open my eyes,
lift my hand, clench my fingers.

They are distant and nearby
behind nine hills
in a secret den.

No one can appease them
in their nocturnal monopoly
or dawn-cloak.

They stay where they are.
In the chest, the heart
from which they murmur.

МАСКЕ

1

У воду је скочио човек-жаба. Црни
ауто вози Великог Мртваца. Из канте
за смеће вири гипсана нога. Слуге
имају бледа лица. Мраз је народни
покривач. Нико не може отпевати
химну. Облак стоји на небу. Муња је
црвена жица. Лава се охладила и
стврдла. Нико ти ништа не може.
Стави кристал под главу и запевај.
Јастребе, оштри нокте. Сечива негуј.
Изнад сваког лица звоне сузне маске.
Сунчеви су зраци змијске ноге. Све
живо је на врховима прстију. Одблескуј,
Ништавило.

MASKS

1

The man-frog jumped into the water. A black car
drives the Big Corpse around. A plaster leg juts
from a dumpster. The pale servants. Frost, the people's
blanket. No one can sing the anthem. A cloud hangs
in the sky. Red wire lightning. The lava has cooled
and hardened. No one can hurt you. Place a crystal
under your head and begin singing. Hawk, sharpen
your talons. Cherish your blades. Over every face
a tragedy mask mourns. The sun hides its head.
Nothingness, keep emanating.

2

Погледај: рађам те као што и ти мене
рађаш. Животиње се камене и силазе
под земљу. Птице су пернате рукавице,
крилата со, знаци. Снег пада у брдима.
Копно је балкон отворен према мору.
Ти се ту појављујеш и шиштиш, пропасти.
Твој је пољубац седми печат, закон над
законима. Ништа поред ничега, прах смо
изнад пустиње. На првом ће нас углу
као сувенире продати. Мумија ће се придићи
да нас благослови. Последњи од нас имаће
беле, преврнуте очи. Јекнуће и посивети
нагло. На плотовима висе скотови, с неба
капљу отрови. Мучитељи већ хрле, жене
Стаклооке.

2

Look: I'm birthing you the way you're birthing
me. Animals turn to stone and descend
underground. Birds are feathered gloves,
winged salt, omens. It's snowing in the hills.
The mainland is a balcony overlooking the sea.
It is here that you appear and wheeze, ruin.
Your kiss is the seventh seal, the law of
laws. We're nothing next to nothing, ashes
over a desert. At the nearest corner we'll be sold
like souvenirs. The Mummy will rise
to bless us. The last of us will look
with upturned eyes. We will shriek and turn
suddenly gray. Beasts hang on the fences, poisons
drip from the sky. Many a Glass-eyed Tormentress
already hastens.

3

Преко мене надолази дно и све
невидљиво надолази. Непомичан
кући путујем. Лукави ме срета
ледом, Бог огњем. Дете у колевци,
мој дух је пријемчив. Носим, ево,
хиљаду и једну лудачку кошуљу.
Видео сам свој леш у лули, дим и
сенку. Опеваће ме само хор лудих
кћери. Чудовишни унуци излазе
из мирисних ковчега. Анђели ће
слетети на олупине, кристали ће се
окретати. Моје су речи прасак,
у мојој је утроби звезда, и то је
знак моје ноћи. Дивота сам ја,
и страх сам. Кукаван у својој
Години.

3

The end and all that's hidden overtake
me. I'm going home in repose.
The Cunning One meets me with ice,
God with flame. My spirit receptive
like a baby in a crib. Here, I'm wearing
1001 straitjackets. I saw my own corpse
in a pipe, becoming smoke and shadow.
Only a choir of mad daughters will eulogize
me. Miraculous grandsons are leaving
scented coffins. Angels will swoop onto scraps,
crystals will spin. My words are thunder,
a star in my gut, a symbol of my night.
I am splendor, and I am fear.
Wretched in my Year.

4

Свако име прихвата и свако одбацује,
Неизрециво. Оно подиже језик према непцима,
поглед према небесима, заустављајући
руку човечју на самом рубу Понора.
У свакој страви оно гледа иза завесе,
у сваком очајању грчи прсте. Оно нади
отвара враташца, а смртне брише трагове.
Оно расеца мреже закона, и указује се
као уништење или чудо. Стар, усамљен,
изгубљен, никакав, у њему се као у дечијој
љуљашци одмарам. Сањарим. Снивам.
Помислим: Боже мој, Ти ниси за собом
сва врата затворио. Ниси ме оставио,
Саваоте.

4

The Unspeakable accepts and rejects
every name. It lifts its tongue toward the palate,
its eyes toward the heavens, stops the human hand
at the very edge of the Abyss. In every horror
it peers from behind a curtain, and in every despair
it clenches its hands. It opens a tiny door to hope
and erases deathly tracks. It tears the net of law,
and appears as destruction or miracle. Being old, lonely,
lost, worthless, I'm resting in it as in a swing. I daydream.
I dream. I think: my God, You did not close all the doors
behind You. You didn't abandon me, Savior.

5

Трбоња и куљавац чисти су
као суза. Доушник и подводач
жуборе као поток планински.
Балегари су истребљени, смрдибубе
мучки побијене. Мечкари се
редовно купају. У мучионицама
опрали су руке мучитељи; уста
и пазуха намирисали су дискретно,
врло дискретно. Добошари су под
земљом, викачи у пречистој води.
Касапи ударце римују, паликуће
у прсте дувају. У забранима егзо-
тичним рајске птице певају умилно.
Из кажњеничких каменолома допире
Песма над песмама.

5

The potbellied and the paunchy are clean
as a whistle. The informant and the pimp
murmur like a mountain brook.
Dung beetles are exterminated, stinkbugs
are savagely killed off. Bear tamers
bathe regularly. In torture chambers,
tormentors wash their hands. They clean
their mouths and armpits discreetly,
very discreetly. Drummers are underground,
and screamers are in all too clean water.
Butchers synchronize their chopping, arsonists
blow on their fingers. Birds of paradise sing
in exotic preserves. From penitentiary quarries
the Song of Songs rises.

МАЧКА

У складишту свих ствари,
она меком шапицом
одгуркује маску
коју придржавам испред лица.

Прозрела је она моју игру.
Нисам јој ни најмање страшан.

Игра се мојом маском,
игра се мојом игром.

THE CAT

In the storage of all things,
she, with a soft little paw,
keeps pushing off the mask
which I hold in front of my face.

She saw through my game.
I'm not in the least terrifying for her.

She's playing with my mask,
playing with my game.

РОДОСЛОВ ЏЕЛАТА

Крволок роди Благога
Благи роди Праведног
Праведни роди Мајстора
Мајстор роди Доктора

Доктор роди Утвару
Утвара роди Господина
Господин роди Гаврана
Гавран роди Славуја

Славуј роди Љубазног
Љубазни роди Пријазног
Пријазни роди Одурног
Одурни роди Пресветлог

Пресветли роди Кобру
Кобра роди Питомог
Питоми роди Шакала
Шакал роди Путника

Путник роди Злотвора
Злотвор роди Лептира
Лептир роди Штиглица
Штиглиц роди Крмачу

THE GENEALOGY OF THE EXECUTIONER

The Blood-guzzler births the Mild One
the Mild One births the Just One
the Just One births the Repairman
the Repairman births the Doctor

the Doctor births the Apparition
the Apparition births the Gentleman
the Gentleman births the Raven
the Raven births the Nightingale

the Nightingale births the Kindly One
the Kindly One births the Amiable One
the Amiable One births the Repulsive One
the Repulsive One births the Most Holy

the Most Holy births the Cobra
the Cobra births the Tame One
the Tame One births the Jackal
the Jackal births the Passenger

the Passenger births the Criminal
the Criminal births the Butterfly
the Butterfly births the Goldfinch
the Goldfinch births the Sow

Крмача роди Зрикавца
Зрикавац роди Зумбула
Зумбул роди Згуреног
Згурени роди Корњачу

Корњача роди Грофа
Гроф роди Хијену
Хијена роди Гусана
Гусан роди Гугутку

Гугутка роди Баука
Баук роди Овчицу
Овчица роди Џелата
Џелат роди Џелата

the Sow births the Cricket
the Cricket births the Hyacinth
the Hyacinth births the Croucher
the Croucher births the Turtle

the Turtle births the Count
the Count births the Hyena
the Hyena births the Gander
the Gander births the Turtledove

the Turtledove births the Bogeyman
the Bogeyman births the Ewe
the Ewe births the Executioner
the Executioner births the Executioner

РЕСИЦА, МИНИФОН

Тај чова-чворак док је праведно спавао
отворених уста, заваљен на лежају,
лакокрили ваздушни дух (ко би други?)
за ресицу му пажљиво веза
још једну будну ћелију – минифон залепи.
Сад ће и његов унутрашњи говор
бити познат: све превратничке намере
и ток немирних мисли биће познати
у танане танчине. Изабранику веселом
само су две ствари остале: да увлачи главу
у рамена, крши прсте, и говори при том
речи похвале и тупе покопности, или да заволи
најдубљу тишину с бесконачним, животом
испод одузетог језика. У пречистом
                                    ходнику Клинике
помолимо се за њега, скрушени уздахнимо.

UVULA, BUGGING DEVICE

While the geezer-starling slept the sleep of the just
sprawled out on the bed
with his mouth open,

a light-winged ghost (who else?)
carefully planted another watchful cell –
glued a bugging device to his uvula.

Now even his internal speech
will be known: all of his revolutionary intentions
and the train of his restless thoughts will be revealed
in minute detail.

Only two choices remain
to the lucky one: to shrug his shoulders,
wring his hands, and all-the-while speak
words of praise in dull submissiveness,

or to grow to love
deathly silence with an overlong life
under a paralyzed tongue.

In the spanking clean
hallways of the Clinic
let's pray for him, sigh a broken sigh.

ЈАБУКА

Расекох јутрос јабуку,
кад тамо:

познати потпис
последњег диктатора.

Небом
       млазњак
бео траг
       оставља.

AN APPLE

I sliced through an apple this morning,
and there it was:

the familiar signature
of the last dictator.

In the sky
        a jet fighter
leaves
        a white trail.

МУВА, 1989.

Бог те под небесима благословио,
мртва муво.

Зинула си преко свог зева
и ниско пала.

Ту где су отворене ране,
твоје је тамно краљевство.

И ти си, године ове,
изнад историје зујкала.

Никад сита, хтела си тамо
као у месару улетети,
напити се с крвавих потока.

На прозорској дасци славно лежиш.

FLY, 1989

May God in heaven bless you,
dead fly.

You gaped wider than your yawn,
fell from grace.

Where open wounds are,
your dark domain lies.

This year, you have
buzzed above history.

Never sated, you just wanted
to fly into the butcher shop
and gorge yourself on bloody streams.

Now, you gloriously lie on the windowsill.

ОКУПАЦИЈА

Све време нешто банално, бесмислено,
а из свега тога
понека искрица кресне, пробије се,
блесне ту и тамо,
као креста украденог петла. А кокоши
кљују лешеве војника
и носе јаја у пепелу. На зидинама.

OCCUPATION

Out of the day-to-day banality, absurdity,
an occasional sparkle glitters, breaks through,
flashes here and there,
like the crest of a stolen rooster. Hens
peck at the corpses of soldiers,
lay eggs in ashes. On the ramparts.

ИЗМЕЂУ ДВЕ САЛВЕ

Између две салве, са радија, крици паунова
из зеленила се вртног огласише. Зафрфљаше
птице-пси. Јер господара њиховог, љубичицу,
сахрањују. А онда: потресни глас спикера,

музика и лирика свих песника тужних поданика
испунише станиште моје пусто где ми дани
теку. Теку куд теку. Теку никуда. И страва,
свудприсутна, још ме једном ови, фабричких
сирена хор кад писну, у заказани туге час.

BETWEEN TWO SALVOS

On the radio, his garden peacocks shriek
between two salvos. Bird-dogs gibber
for their master, their violet, laid to rest.
The somber voice of the announcer, the music
and the verses of poets, his saddened subjects,

fill my barren den where my days drift by.
They go where they go: nowhere.
And terror, omnipresent, consumes me
when the choir of the factory sirens sound
at the scheduled hour of mourning.

БИОГРАФИЈА

Викао сам: Немојте мене тући,
рођен сам у сиромашној породици.
Али то ништа није помогло,
полицајци си ударали све жешће.
По ребрима и леђима, свој ски,
дописивали су моју биографију.
Сад могу рећи, уз смешак:
Рођен сам у сиромашној породици,
пребијала ме полиција...
Али, свакога се, данас, клоним.
Највише људи с оскудним
биографијама, почетника клетих.
Дођу тако, причају којешта,
околише и слатко се облизују.
Траже оно што им никако не могу дати.

BIOGRAPHY

I shouted, "Don't beat me –
I was born into a poor family!"
But that didn't help.
The police hit me all the more;
on my ribs and back, relentlessly,
fleshing out my biography.

Now I can say, with a smile,
"I was born into a poor family,
the police brutalized me."

But these days I shy away from everyone.
Mostly people with scant biographies,
the damned novices.
They bother me with their nonsense
licking their lips. They're looking
for what I can't give them.

КОНГРЕС (ФАНТАЗМА)

Сви сабрани дуси света
хомоиди страшни
изнад опширних реферата подижу
прсте с атомским главама

О биће заиста за све
црног млека крваве чоколаде
тајанствених подрума влажних
и дубоких јама с лавовима

Још кад сине светлост са небеса
отвориће нам се очи
видећемо бездан
само тамно промицање

ASSEMBLY (PHANTASM)

The shadows of the world assembled
horrible humanoids
gesticulating with warheads
over their lengthy reports

there will certainly be for everyone
black milk, bloody chocolate,
mysterious damp basements
and deep pits with lions

and when the light shines from above
our eyes will open
and we'll see the abyss:
a grim procession

СТРАХ

Укочен као лутка, не знам више
с које ће стране зло стићи.
Гле, на лакту ми се око отворило.

FEAR

Stiff as a doll, I'm not sure any more
from where evil will come.
Look, on my elbow an eye has opened.

БРОЈАНИЦА (ПРОТИВ УТВАРА)

Они нису људи.
Само се праве да су људи.

Они нису кактуси.
Само се праве да су кактуси.

Они нису мачке.
Само се праве да су мачке.

Они нису птице.
Само се праве да су птице.

Они нису сенке.
Само се праве да су сенке.

Они лете на ветру.
Они скачу по крововима.
Они су утваре у ноћи.

INCANTATION (AGAINST PHANTOMS)

They're not human –
only pretending to be human.

They're not cacti –
only pretending to be cacti.

They're not cats –
only pretending to be cats.

They're not birds –
only pretending to be birds.

They're not shadows –
only pretending to be shadows.

They're carried by the wind.
They leap over rooftops.
They're night phantoms.

III

ИЗЛОЖБА

Кована авет на постољу
у савременој галерији

У најтврђем камену
уловљена сабласт птицолика

Неко непознато чудовиште
на једној нози стоји
савијајући врх репа у уста

На лицу дрвене статуе
урезан мој плач
којим се први пут
у свету огласих

Од металних отпадака витез
подигао мач зарђали да ме брани

EXHIBITION

In a gallery of contemporary art:
a forged apparition on a pedestal

A bird-faced specter
captured in the hardest stone

A strange monster
standing on one foot
bends the tip of its tail into its mouth

Tears that first announced me
to the world are engraved
on the face of a wooden statue

A knight of metal scraps
raises his rusty sword to defend me

ЗАСТАВА

Цела баш се породица
ту сабрала
контејнеру на рамена
црни тата, краста-мама, костур-дете
са кесама, са врећама
да пецају пецароши
па детенце спустили су
тамо на дно, усред
смећа
а оно је крвав тампон подигнуло
ко заставу
понижених

ништа
више.

FLAG

The whole family gathers
by the rim of a trash bin
wretched dad, scabby mom, skeleton kid
fish with plastic bags and sacks
like fishermen
so dad and mom lower the tyke
to the bottom of the garbage
and he picks up a bloody tampon
a flag
of the humiliated

nothing
more.

ФОТОГРАФИЈА

Неки човек окренут леђима
стоји поред зида
мокри
види се у благом луку
млаз потопне воде
како пада у смеће
поред ципела његових

Фотографија је
на картону залепљена
и обешена
као икона
на косом зиду твоје собе
самртниче бледи

THE PHOTOGRAPH

A man with his back turned
faces a wall
urinates
the jetting arc
a deluge
onto the garbage
next to his shoes

The photograph
mounted on cardboard
hangs
like an icon
on the slanted wall of your room,
ashen face

СВЕСКА, ГЛАС

Без икакве мисли у глави,
седео је у празној соби.

„Људи су нечисти створови“,
записао је недавно у свесци
на коју је, лако, положио руку.

Изненада поче да броји
прсте на отвореној шаци.

Кад их преброја, сети се
да већ трећи дан није чуо
глас мртве мајке са радија.

NOTEBOOK, VOICE

A man sat without a thought
in an empty room.

His hand rested on his notebook.

He had recently written:
"People are impure creatures."

He began counting on his fingers.

It'd been three days since he last heard
the voice of his dead mother from the radio.

УДОВИЦА

Она је буђ која расте
на влажној подлози.

Ту где је сада
не постоји нико други.

Мужа је имала и немала;
деце је имала и немала;
среће је имала и немала.

Преподневни је час
и она лежи у кухињи.

Прозор је отворен; њише се
пожутела прозорска завеса.

Као за пакост, сунце сија
и расипа се свеколико благо божије.

THE WIDOW

She is the mold growing
in the damp foundation.

No one else exists
where she is now.

She had a husband and didn't have a husband;
had children and didn't have children;
luck and no luck.

In the morning,
she lies down in the kitchen.

The window is open;
the yellowed curtain billows.

As if in spite, the sun shines
and scatters its divine wealth.

ЈА И ТИ

То сам ја, само кост и кожа,
поред шумског пута.

Река крви и снова
текла је
и кроз моје тело.

То сам ја са којим си
једном
жучно расправљао
а сад ме
не познајеш.

Док речи ти звоне,
охоло главу подижеш.

Решио си све загонетке,
и процветао у својој сили.

YOU AND I

That's me, just skin and bones,
by a wooded path.

A river of blood and dreams
also coursed
through my body.

That's me
we once bitterly argued
but now you don't recognize me.

As your words resound,
you raise your haughty head.

You solved all the riddles,
and blossomed in your might.

СОНЕТ МРТВИХ СОВА

(O) (O) (O) (O) (O)
(O) (O) (O) (O) (O)
(O) (O) (O) (O) (O)
(O) (O) (O) (O) (O)

(O) (O) (O) (O) (O)
(O) (O) (O) (O) (O)
(O) (O) (O) (O) (O)
(O) (O) (O) (O) (O)

никада више никуда
никада више никуда
никада више никуда

никада више никуда
никада више никуда
никада више никуда

SONNET OF DEAD OWLS

(O) (O) (O) (O) (O)
(O) (O) (O) (O) (O)
(O) (O) (O) (O) (O)
(O) (O) (O) (O) (O)

(O) (O) (O) (O) (O)
(O) (O) (O) (O) (O)
(O) (O) (O) (O) (O)
(O) (O) (O) (O) (O)

nowhere ever again
nowhere ever again
nowhere ever again

nowhere ever again
nowhere ever again
nowhere ever again

IV

КЕЗИЛОВ ДОЛАЗАК

Подземно би сада
Кроз брежуљак топли
Моја грижо покренута ситнежи
На теби је да надјачаш
Слепљену тишину и да се
На зид обли као на заћуткану
Страст у добри час устремиш
Врата да шкрипну и разнесу
Заточеника и сиви његов ваздух
Ево у шркињу је већ приспео
У питомину млаку и чупаву
Одакле потмуло прокљувава
Једну једину ногу да продене
Стоног хоће да ми дође
Да се у црницу до појаса порине
Ивицом скученог света
Ужагрен оптрчава

MOCKERATOR'S ARRIVAL

Guilt, gather giblets
beneath the fresh mound
Overpower the thick silence
Burrow under the stone slab
Let the lid creak and crush me,
the captive, and my gray air
Come into the trunk
from the warm tangled earth
Peck your way in
Slip in one leg after another
Enter like an eager centipede
through the loam toward me
Smolder along the edge
of my cramped world

ИЗА РУЖИЧЊАКА КЕЗИЛО

Иза ружичњака дрвеће шумори
Кргаче пуни из тајних бунара
Сумњив оброк

Тамни лик лукаво врата отвара
Испод црне клеке излази
Из сребрног лишћа вреба

На врат ће ми скочити
Дрвеће кад га целог изнесе

Његов је корак
И то тихо кретање обрве
Коју померам до сред чела

MOCKERATOR BEHIND THE ROSE GARDEN

Trees rustle behind the rose garden
Pails fill up from secret wells
A suspicious meal

A dark shape slyly opens the door
Comes from underneath the black juniper tree
Lurks among silver leaves

He will lunge for my throat
when the trees expel him

His swift stride
My eyebrows knit
the middle of my forehead

КЕЗИЛОВА ПОЈАВА НА ПРСТИМА

Црно козле дај ми црне рогове
А ви девојчице дајте ми
Влажне трубе
         Како бих заплашио
Оног који се развезује

Црно козле дај ми ледне очи
А ви девојчице прва огледалца
Да већ нешто у рукама имам
Јер његов се лик распиње
Преко моје шаке
Моје шаке разгранате у прсте

MOCKERATOR'S APPEARANCE ON FINGERS

Black goat, give me your black horns
and you girls, give me
damp trumpets
        so that I may frighten
the one untying himself

Black goat, give me your icy eyes
and you girls, give me your first compact mirrors
so I'll have something in my palms
as his face unfurls
across my hand
branching into my fingers

ФЛАША КЕЗИЛО

Издужена лика
У флаши клокоћеш
Давиш се можда
Водена твоја
Коса
У грлу ми
Певуши
     Опет
Опет си ту
О дебелоусни
Уоколо за нас
Нико не зна

BOTTLE-MOCKERATOR

Long-faced
you gurgle in the bottle
perhaps drowning
Your watery hair
cooing in my throat
                    again
Again, you're here
Oh, fat-lipped one
nobody around us
knows about us

БОКАЛ КЕЗИЛО

Бокал је шкрто појило
Улудо му бокове натежем
Студена стегна
Око зато наднесох
Где кезило склупчани
У воду сламку умочио
Па лагано пије
Све што ван је бокала
То галами и жагору
Припада
Шапну он свету на домаку

PITCHER-MOCKERATOR

The pitcher is a stingy watering hole
I take a swig in vain
squeezing its hips
its cold thighs
I peep into the hole
Behold the mockerator curled up
sipping water
through a straw
He whispers to the world at his fingertips
Everything beyond the pitcher
belongs to racket
and murmur

ЛОНАЦ КЕЗИЛО

Клемпавку
Облоглавом је шешир
У плафон полетео
Соба је из уста штрцнула
Пребогат је видим
Тесно му је
Јер ваздух сеже плитко
Тражи да руке уроним
Како би се уз њих
Сав шљам
Што су га баш оне ту сасуле
Узверао

POT-MOCKERATOR

The lop-eared one's hat
shot up from his round head
The room within
squirted from his mouth
I can tell he's too full
he's cramped
gasping for air
urging me
to submerge my hands
so all the scum
they dumped
can climb up

ЈАБУКА ЈЕ КЕЗИЛОВА

Сведочи да је на сто из тамне пала
Крошње у којој гавран кљун оштри

Утврди у њој затечену ситнеж што се
При одгризу показује а здрава памет

Мисли да је то своју вилицу одсликала
Па се зато не знајући коме осмехује

EVEN THE APPLE BELONGS TO THE MOCKERATOR

It claims to have fallen onto the table
from the underdark of treetops

where a raven strops its beak
Biting into the apple giblets burst forth

Teeth marks show it's smiling
but doesn't know at whom

ПОРЦУЛАН КЕЗИЛО

Као јаре у оскудан крш
У порцелан си сатеран
Или си тамо
Изван смешних збрка
У предугом предаху
Кезило из белог хлада
Гледај како ми низ браду и прса
Свет цури
Непрестано
На мене сикћеш
А из свог предела не излазиш

PORCELAIN-MOCKERATOR

Like a billy goat on rocky ground
you've been driven
into the porcelain's deep recess
beyond the absurd clutter
Mockerator, from your white shade
watch the world dribble
down my chin and chest
incessantly
You're hissing at me
but remain in your niche

СПАЛА ЈЕ САПУНИЦА

Видео сам те како си
Низ улицу долазио

Видео сам те међу онима
Који те не познају

Намештао си им боре
И неке ствари журно
На гомилу бацао

Спала је блага сапуница
Обезбеђен је простор за тебе

Видео сам те међу голим гранама

SOAPSUDS SLID OFF

I saw you
coming down the street

I saw you
among those who don't know you

You shaped their wrinkles
and hastily threw some things onto a pile

Sparse soapsuds slid off
A space freed up for you

I saw you
among bare branches

У ПОСУЂУ КЕЗИЛО

Као да неко плаче
Као да неко посуђе пере
Служавко
Где се сада крпе цеде
Са каквог конопца
Гроб ти не озелене
Већ према мени
Црну главу подиже
Свеже раме
У руци мемлу држиш
Која би ми помогла
Звонке ствари око мене
Која би растурила
Али ти храниш
Мале кезилиће
И овог овде што се
Из посуђа церека

MOCKERATOR IN THE DISHES

As if someone's weeping
As if someone's washing dishes
Maid, from what clothesline
are the rags hanging now
Your grave hasn't yet greened
but raises its black head to me
Fresh shoulder
your hand holds the dankness
which could help me
break the clinking dishes
about me
Instead you are feeding
newborn mockerators –
that one there
snickers from the dishes

КЕЗИЛИЋИ

Кевтаве губице
У порубима и шавовима
Ситнеж балава

Мицала гладна мицала
Разроких језика
Иверје похотно

Под зањиханим смрекама
Сечива и сисала
Лизала мљацкала кусала

Телоточци и растакала
Ужурбана око мене
Мала клапкала

NEWBORN MOCKERATORS

Yelping muzzles,
slobbery giblets
in hems and seams,

probing hungry probers,
twisted tongues,
voracious splinters

under swaying juniper trees,
sucklings and chisels,
lickers, chompers, relishers,

fleshstreamers and diluters,
small tappers
rushing around me

СМРТ У СТОЛИЦИ

Сад су све репатице отиснуте
низ твоје чело
испод крика као да ништа није остало
ништа ти више не шапуће
ту си само да стршиш
уосталом доста је било ломатања
док опет не чујеш
оно пуцкетање оно подземно
неподношљиво незадовољство
лези у муклу носиљку
до сићушне душе зури
ово је послеподневни одмор
када су далеко сва приземља
на тебе је зинуло средиште
реци да ти донесу чашу воде
ту су чисти одблесци и севања
но ти ћеш их сада превидети
јер мраз је стиснуо зенице
на високима и у доловима могу без тебе
не маме те не приклањај се зато
не завијај не цичи не гарави
не вери се и не хрли
сустао си опкољен пратњом

DEATH IN THE CHAIR

Comets have now run
down your forehead;
a shriek, as if nothing remained.
Nothing whispers to you anymore.
You are left here trembling.
Enough floundering
until you hear again
crackling deep within
the unbearable discontent.
Rest in the silent sedan chair, and
gaze into the tiny soul.
This is an afternoon nap,
the ground is distant.
Your core gapes at you.
Tell someone to bring you a glass of water
with gleams and flashes.
Still, you'll lose sight of them
as frost hardens your pupils.
Peaks and valleys exist without you,
they're not luring you.
Don't howl, don't scream, don't con,
don't climb, don't rush.
Your wearying entourage,

злим поворкама којим
блиски амбис настани
о то је само пошкропљена гибељ
што на дно тебе испод грабежљиве
куке оног који те заклања беше сложена
свет у мишијој рупи то беше
свет испод трна
а сад отпоздрављај маши
већ си опако преплануо од своје склоности
или још чекаш у јазбини
гледаш из невоље и покоре из шушкора
чекаш ма какву настраност
па да ти се љуте носнице рашире
да спустиш прст обележиш пукотину
много је ипак њих превише је њих
погледај само тај масив пред прозором
тло на коме паде
или се сети драге своје свеколике
присети се вашег првог сусрета
када ти рече да си рашчерупан петао
рече и побеже
према крововима према великом бусењу
а ти си свакодневно јео мрачну грмљавину
на прагу те је чекао верно разговор
са самим собом ту ћеш рећи

an evil procession where
the nearby abyss resides –
just bespattered bodies
stacked within you, under the angling
hook of the one obscuring you;
that used to be a world in a mouse hole,
a world underneath a thorn.
And now, wave goodbye;
your habits tan you.
Are you still in your lair
peering from your rustling, trouble and submission
waiting for any perversity?
Your nostrils flare
as you trace cracks with your finger.
There are many of them, too many of them.
Just look at that massif outside your window
the ground on which you've fallen
or remember your dear being
recall your first encounter
when it called you a ruffled rooster
and fled
toward the roofs, toward the great clumps of earth
and you ate black thunder every day.
On the threshold,
the usual conversation

да највећа сласт је да нас нема
на овој узвисини тише само тише
овде последњи пут зазиваш
много је њих превише је њих
много скакутана много кезила
и свеколика твоја загасита твоја
и њено рубље које је пуно црних петлова
и њене шнале које корачају улицом
много је њих превише је њих
превелик је брат твој кезило
и послужитељ твој кезило
много је њих превише је њих
столица се твоја растресла у сто лица
у столик
дело је твоје завршено столица се
у стоногу претворила
отпоздрављај само маши маши дуго
највећа сласт је да нас нема
реци најзад какви су твоји изгледи
јер лепо си се узаслонио
реп подвио кљун загњурио
у намргођено перје
као да се чистиш као да се растајеш
док дан спрам тебе пружа свој длан провидни

with yourself. You said
that the greatest delight is when we are no more.
On this peak, quiet down, just quiet down;
for the last time you're calling out.
There are many of them, too many of them.
Many Hoppingers, many Mockerators.
And your darkness
with its laundry full of black roosters
and its barrettes marching down the street.
There are many of them, too many of them.
Your Brother-mockerator is colossal,
and the Server, your Mockerator, too.
There are many of them, too many of them.
Your chair has been split into a hundred faces
into a hundred-faced one.
Your deed is done. The chair has
turned into a centipede.
Wave goodbye. Just wave, keep waving.
The greatest joy is when we're no more.
Say at last what your prospects are
because you have found something to lean against.
You tucked your tail between your legs, and
you buried your beak
into your ruffled feathers
as if you were cleaning yourself, as if you were leaving
while the day offers its transparent palm to you.

AB OVO

У родном зиду у даљини
с оне стране ствари и језика
склупчан док се будиш
од тебе моћни створе
на вртном дрвету лишће дрхти
и мрачна жестина допире одасвуд
јер ти си дојенче и старац
и крвави чавао што из прашине се подиже

И овде изнад постеље умирућег
јавља се огромно округло
жарким прстењем напуњено
кристалима прамаглином напуњено
узнемирено зажагрено
јавља се твоје око врховне Кокошке

Кад ваздух на мртво лице налаже
кад се више живи облици не смењују
кад је све уништено отклоњено
отвара се ноћу твоје пуно писмо

AB OVO

In the birth wall, in the distance
beyond matter and language
you wake curled up, fearsome creature
the leaves of the garden tree tremble
a shadowy rage reaches from everywhere
you are a suckling, an old man,
a bloody nail rising from the dust

Above the deathbed
an enormous round shape appears
holds burning rings
holds ancient crystal mist
disturbed, smoldering,
your eye opens, Arch Hen

When the air settles on the dead face
when living shapes no longer change
when all that's destroyed has been removed
at night your entire message hatches

РИТУАЛ

Паклена бебо
под земљом си ти
јаје си ти
склупчана енергија си ти
јаје си ти
притајена енергија си ти
паклена бебо
јаје се ти

претња си јаје си
страшно си јаје си
крајње си јаје си
изрод си јаје си
крајње си јаје си
страшно си јаје си
претња си јаје си

врати се богу Кокоши
врати се богу Кокоши

RITUAL

Infernal baby
underground you are
egg you are
curled up energy you are
egg you are
hidden energy you are
egg you are
infernal baby

threat you are – egg you are
horrible you are – egg you are
abject you are – egg you are
freak you are – egg you are
abject you are – egg you are
horrible you are – egg you are
threat you are – egg you are

return to god, Hen
return to god, Hen

КОКОТУША

Дружино ноћна дружино
Грбоњице и губаљи
Крвопилци и кусаљи
И сви остали и ви остали

Наша је света мајка
Наша је нова богиња
Усред селца селцета
Пламене кресте кокотуша

У овом часу алавом
У овом трену окатом
Истина је сушта истина
Све што о њој слажемо

CLUCKER

Horde, nocturnal horde
Petite hunchbacks and lepers
Bloodsuckers and short-tailed ones
And all of the others and the rest of you

The holy mother is ours
The new goddess is ours
In the midst of a little village, a tiny village
Fiery-crested clucker

At this voracious hour
At this keen-sighted moment
Truth is bare truth
All that we lie about

КОКОШ У СОБИ

од ормана до врата
дрвено сам легло попречио
под њеним прљавим присуством
ствари да уздрхте

свакодневно узбирам
продевене перјем
пепељасте хрпице

јаје кад снесе позваћу пријатеље
да га с длетима отворимо
или да га из куће изгурамо

њу не видим
иако собни простор
квоца и узмахује
да ми ваздух лице шиба

кад цигарете или прсте запаљујем
креста се на шибици јави

HEN IN THE ROOM

underneath her filthy presence
I built a wooden nest
from the wardrobe to the door
everything shakes

every day I collect
little ashen feathers
with jutting quills

I call my friends when she lays an egg
to crack it open with chisels
or roll it out of the house

I don't see her
though the room
is clucking and flapping
my face is wing-whipped

when I light up a cigarette or my fingers
her crest appears on the match

ГЛЕДАМ

у колутовима дима
видим жути језик

видим ћубастог копца
како се устремљује

AS I WATCH

through smoke rings
I see a yellow tongue

a crested sparrow hawk
swoops down

РАДНИ СТО

на столу мирују канџасте руке

на папирима необрађене
још у топлим парама изнутрице

прозор је најзад сунуо
мириси моји ветре

и врата отвара

утвара

DESK

clawed hands rest on the desk

fresh innards
steam on the page

the window bursts open
and my scent airs out

nudging the door –

the apparition

БОР

бор расте у слици на зиду
према мени гране њише

по поду иглице падају
зид кокош храни

смоле у запис капају
реч за реч лепе

мој нови строј мирише
и борову сенку
продужава, кроз несану ноћ

PINE TREE

the pine tree grows in the wall painting
reaching its branches toward me

needles fall to the floor
the wall feeds the hen

sap drips onto the writing
gluing word to word

oil smell of my new typewriter
the pine tree's shadow
lengthens through the sleepless night

СТОЛЊАК

на стољњаку чипке
изнутрице заклане живине

узалуд га отресам
чипке не отпадају

у углу извезена риба
чврсто за реп ухваћена

TABLECLOTH

innards of slaughtered poultry
on the lace tablecloth

I'm shaking them out in vain
the stitching doesn't come off

along the hem, an embroidered fish –
its tail trapped

ЗАВЕСЕ

као стрељани завесе се
низ прозоре и зидове спузавају

у мождане наборе
намештај да увију

тада баш кокош
око нежних младих јаја коре чврсне

CURTAINS

as if after a firing squad, the curtains
slump against the walls and windows

like brain furrows
to drape the furniture

the hen hardens the shells
of her fragile young eggs

НАХТКАСНА

не смем је отворити
јер би оживели рукописи
са зглавкастим удовима
отпочели несавршено
гибање густог ваздуха
и зидови би се собни искосили

у померeним би се угловима
кокош нахранила
под пуном вољом
несносно подне греје

плафон се у бело перје раздели

NIGHTSTAND

I dare not open it
or the awakened manuscripts
would awkwardly stretch their arthropod limbs
in stale air
the walls of the room would close in

in tightening corners
the hen would gorge herself
in the unbearable afternoon

the ceiling would open up onto white feathers

ЛУТАЈУЋИ ОГАЊ

Лутајући огањ, нечији
расечени вео.

Ако ме дотакне, нестаћу
у најтежим мукама,

без трага, у трен.

WANDERING FIRE

Wandering fire, someone's
    cut up veil.

If it touches me, I'll vanish
    in agony,

without a trace, instantly.

СВЕЋА

Црна мисао
(зломисао)
око глежњева
омотала ми се,
на врат скочила,
у срце сишла.
Мој добри
анђео чувар
ту је за крај
ухватио, и огњем
небеским,
преблагим
заждио.
Сад гори
моја свећа,
усправљена
у мом мраку,
и мене посрнулог
усправља.

CANDLE

Black thought
(illthought)
coils around
my ankles,
lunges
at my throat,
descends
into my heart.
My guardian
angel grabs
the candle,
lights it
so gently
with holy
fire. My candle
burns upright
in my gloom.
I, the stumbling
man, now upright.

My favorite poem

135

BIBLIOGRAPHY

Novica Tadić (1949-   )

Presences (*Prisustva*) (1974)
Death in the Chair (*Smrt u stolici*) (1975)
Maw (*Ždrelo*) (1981)
Fiery Hen (*Ognjena kokoš*) (1982)
Wicked Tongue * (*Pogani jezik*) (1984)
The Object of Ridicule ^ (*Ruglo*) (1987)
Poems (*Pesme*) (1988; expanded 1989) – selected poems
About the Brother, Sister and a Cloud (*O bratu, sestri i oblaku*)
    (1989; expanded 1999)
Street (*Ulica*) (1990)
Sparrow Hawk (*Kobac*) (1990)
End of the Year: Grotesques (*Kraj godine : groteske*)
    (1990; expanded 1993) – selected and new poems
Temptation+ (*Napast*) (1994; 2001)
Vagabond (*Potukač*) (1994)
Street and Vagabond (*Ulica and Potukač*) (1999) – collects two
    books and new poems
Unnecessary Companions (*Nepotrebni saputnici*) (1999)
Nocturnal Suites (*Noćna sveta*) (2000) – collects
    Wicked Tongue and *The Object of Ridicule*
Shelter# (*Okrilje*) (2001)

Hoppingers and Mockerators (*Skakutani i kezila*) (2002) –
    collects *Presences* and *Death in the Chair*
Maw (*Ždrelo*) (2002) – collects trilogy *Maw*, *Fiery Hen*
    and *Sparrow Hawk*
Dark Things (*Tamne stvari*) (2003)
The Unknown (*Neznan*) (2006)
Wandering Fire (*Lutajući oganj*) (2007) – selected poems
Devil's Companion (*Davolov drug*) (2008)

English translations:

Night Mail: Selected Poems – translated by Charles Simic (1992)
Dark Things – translated by Charles Simic (2009)
Assembly – translated by Steven Teref and Maja Teref (2009)

notes:
*   alternately translated as *Foul Language*
^   could alternately be translated as *Eyesore*
+   could alternately be translated as *Misery* or *Monster*
#   could be translated as *Wing* or *Protection*

Novica Tadić was born in Smriječno, a small Montenegrin village, in 1949 and lives in Zemun, Serbia. Until 2007, he was the editor-in-chief for the literary publisher Rad, where he worked for 38 years. A renowned Serbian poet and a member of the Serbian Literary Society, he has published sixteen books of poetry, in addition to many selected works. His most recent collection is *Devil's Companion* (2008). His poetry has been represented in many poetry anthologies from Serbia and around the world. Collections of his work have been translated into numerous languages.

Steven Teref, originally from Somerville, MA, teaches literature and writing at Columbia College Chicago. He received his M.F.A. in Poetry from Columbia College Chicago and his B.A. in English from the University of Illinois at Chicago where he also studied Serbo-Croatian under the tutelage of Serbian linguist Biljana Šljivić-Šimšić. His own poems have appeared in *Court Green*, *Black Clock*, *Apocryphal Text* and elsewhere. He is the Technology Chair of IL TESOL (Illinois Teachers of English to Speakers of Other Languages).

Maja Teref, originally from Belgrade, Serbia, worked as a translator, newscaster, and DJ in the English Department at Radio Yugoslavia in the early 1990's. Her B. A. is in English Studies from Belgrade University, and her M.A. is in Applied Linguistics from the University of Illinois at Chicago. She teaches in Chicago and is the 2009-10 President of IL TESOL (Illinois Teachers of English to Speakers of Other Languages).